Blueprint for Strategic Growth

Blueprint for Strategic Growth

Don Kelly, Ph.D.

ISBN 978-0-557-51243-0

Contents

Introduction

This book provides a simple yet highly effective approach for strategically growing your business. Although there are many good books available that describe strategic planning and business development, most offer processes that are extremely detailed and complex. Today's business environment demands that companies maintain a solid vision, coupled with an agile strategic plan and execution process, which can be developed over a short period of time and adapted regularly as business factors change. Simplifying planning and business processes, maximizing precious bid and proposal dollars, and enabling quick responses in your overall business operations puts you in the best position to thrive in a highly dynamic business environment.

This book offers a streamlined yet comprehensive set of tools for doing exactly this. It focuses on providing a solid basis for agile strategic planning and business development.

The planning processes described in this book are directed primarily toward service-oriented companies. Most of the material, however, is also directly applicable to product-based companies.

Why are the planning methods outlined in this book so critical to business success? This book addresses needs in four important business areas. First, there has been an ever-increasing need for cost containment in recent years. In fact, many large bids are now placing more emphasis on cost containment than on the bidder's management and technical approaches. Although this change is somewhat subtle and has been occurring over a number years, it is nonetheless of extreme importance. Companies must now aggressively look for new means to lower or make better use of their overhead costs, especially those relating to bid and proposal. The planning and strategy methods discussed in this book will greatly aid in helping to find and implement cost saving measures.

Second, firms are constantly seeking ways to increase workforce productivity. Companies that do this well realize the efficiencies that can be gained with a well-thought-out corporate strategy. The strategic plan that results will allow both management and employees to be on the same page, with a clear and concise focus on what needs to be done to achieve the firm's vision. Alignment of the corporate strategy and the business development plan offers great potential for saving time and money. This is what strategic growth is all about.

Third, executive teams are often spread too thin. CEOs now must spend even more time on issues that were less important and time-consuming in past years. Legal issues, such as lawsuits and litigation, are just one example. I often hear, "We're too busy to plan, but we know it's essential for our successful growth." This book provides the tools for executive teams to quickly and efficiently conduct their corporate strategy and business development planning.

Finally, there is the link between business success and corporate planning. The research of noted MIT economist, David Birch, shows that 50 percent of businesses fail in the first five years. The figure below shows Birch's calculated business success rates over a ten-year period.[i]

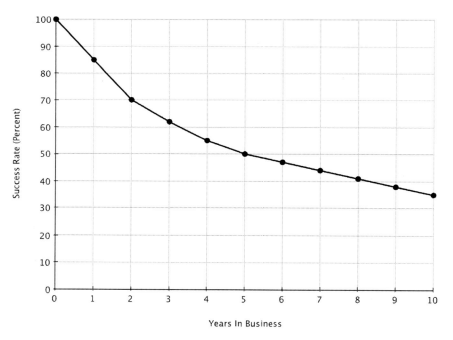

Figure I.1 Ten-Year Business Success Rates

Other research shows comparable findings.

> According to the U.S. Small Business Administration (SBA), roughly half of all businesses fail within the first five years.[ii]

> 64.2% of the businesses failed in a 10-year period.[iii]

> The National Federation of Independent Business estimates that over the lifetime of a business, 39% are

profitable, 30% break even, and 30% lose money, with 1% falling in the 'unable to determine' category.[iv]

Two-thirds of new businesses survive for at least two years, and only 44 percent survive at least four years.[v]

Professor Scott Shane, Case Western Reserve University, reports in his study that only 29% of businesses were still alive after 10 years.[vi]

What causes the extraordinarily high business failure rate, and what can businesses do to not only survive but to succeed? Research has shown that the single biggest contributor to business failure is inadequate business planning.

Research indicates that poor planning is responsible for most business failures.[vii]

Addressing these four important business areas is what this book is all about. Proper strategic and business development planning are the keys to business success and growth. To survive and grow, businesses need to have focused plans that are synchronized with one another.

Strategic growth results from carefully aligning the business opportunities you pursue to your business strategy. In today's extremely fast-paced world, ensuring that new opportunities are carefully aligned to corporate strategy is the most effective way for managing your limited time, maximizing your business development dollars, and pursuing opportunities that you are best positioned to win.

The process of aligning business opportunities to corporate strategy involves the creation and synchronization of four operating plans. These four plans are the Strategic Plan, the Business Development Plan, the Capture Plan, and the Proposal Plan. We will develop each of these by sequentially going over the essential elements for each plan.

A company's strategy addresses the questions, "Who are we and where do we want to go?" The Strategic Plan answers these questions by looking at big picture issues such as the company's vision, values, long and short-term goals, core competencies, strengths, and weaknesses. These issues are especially important in getting the management team and the employees aligned in a single direction with a single purpose.

The business development process starts with the corporate strategy and then addresses the question, "How are we going to grow our business with new opportunities and how will we keep our current business?" The Business Development Plan is the tool for managing the bid and proposal funds, for developing and maintaining customer relationships, for positioning the company for new opportunities, and for bidding on new opportunities.

Once the business development team decides to pursue an opportunity, they need to take two steps. First, they need to determine exactly how to position themselves for winning the opportunity. This is called the capture phase, and the Capture Plan is created to accomplish this step. Second, they need to create a proposal for securing the opportunity. A Proposal Plan is developed to create the winning proposal.

To repeat, the four plans needed for successful and effective strategic growth are the Strategic Plan, the Business Development Plan, the Capture Plan, and the Proposal Plan. Before we get into the essential elements of each of these plans, let's go over the big picture of how they relate to one another.

How to Use This Book

My intent for this book is different than for most other strategic planning and business development books. This book is meant to be a practical, hands-on guide that helps you through the planning process in a logical and meaningful manner.

Rather than just presenting the planning process, I believe it is more helpful to break up plans into their individual components, which I call *Essential Elements*. Many companies do their planning on a quarterly basis, so the Essential Elements provide the executive team with exactly what is needed to develop or update the plans.

Many of the Essential Elements are presented in a template form, with space provided to write in your responses. Others present points to discuss, or require that certain information be gathered or researched.

Once you have addressed each of the Essential Elements for a particular plan, you can assemble them in a notebook and that will be your completed plan. For the Strategic Plan, however, I also provide a special template called the Single-Sheet Strategic Plan. This is a very handy quick reference summary of your Strategic Plan.

You can also go to my Web site (www.trustencore.com) to download free articles, as well as an electronic copy of the Single-Sheet Strategic Plan template. Please see the "Free Templates, Download Instructions" page at the end of this book for downloading instructions.

Chapter 1

The Big Picture

Developing and implementing corporate strategy usually falls upon the shoulders of the chief executive officer (CEO). Because of increasing time demands on CEOs, more and more companies are now adding chief strategy officers (CSOs) to the executive team to assist with corporate strategy.

While the focus of this book is on strategy relating to growth and business, the corporate strategy must encompass all components of the business. These components can vary slightly from company to company and industry to industry. A typical company, for example, might have the following executives with their associated responsibilities:

- CEO—responsible for corporate strategy

- CSO—responsible for oversight and implementation of corporate strategy

- Chief operations officer (COO)—responsible for operations, programs

- Chief finance officer (CFO)—responsible for finance

- Business development director (BD)—responsible for business development and growth

- Human relations director (HR)—responsible for human relations

- Chief information officer (CIO) or information technology director (IT)— responsible for information technology and infrastructure

Whereas the CEO, with support from the CSO, is responsible for corporate strategy, each of the other officers must determine how they are going to execute the corporate strategic goals that relate to their particular areas of responsibility. These plans (Figure 1.1) are necessarily more tactical in nature, but must be closely synchronized with the corporate strategic plan. We will touch upon these different areas in the strategic planning discussion, but again, the focus of this book is primarily on strategic growth and business development.

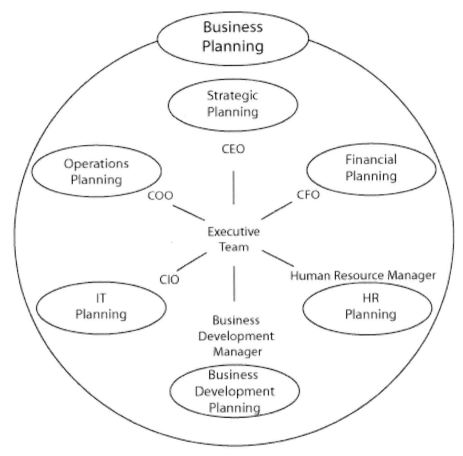

Figure 1.1 Business Planning Components

In order to be highly successful in growing your business, four areas of planning are necessary. These four areas are strategy, business development, capture, and proposals. When targeting a particular opportunity, successful companies often spend 50 to 60 percent of their business development funds prior to the proposal phase. If a company burns through too much of its allocated budget prior to the proposal phase, the odds of winning that opportunity are very low.

Successful companies balance their time and resources across all four planning areas. The figure below shows how strategy guides business development, which guides capture, which guides proposal planning.

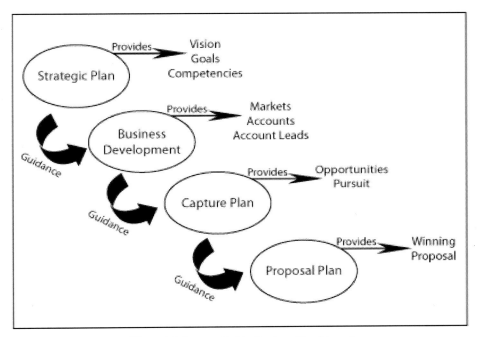

Figure 1.2 Strategy Guides Business Development

Another important point is to understand how the plans relate to each other over time. The Strategic and Business Development Plans are continual, on-going documents. The Strategic Plan is often the responsibility of the CEO or president, and is typically updated quarterly. The Business Development Plan is often the responsibility of the vice-president for business development, or his or her equivalent, and is also typically updated quarterly.

The Capture and Proposal Plans, however, are initiated once an opportunity has been given a *Pursuit Go* from the business development planning process. Once the Pursuit Go has been given, a capture manager and a proposal manager are assigned, and they create the Capture and Proposal Plans, respectively. Thus, the Capture and Proposal Plans are specific to each opportunity, and there may be multiple, on-going Capture and Proposal Plans at any time. The figure below shows how this might look over time.

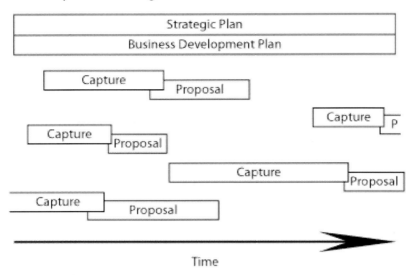

Figure 1.3 Time-Phasing of Strategy and Business Development

The next four chapters will cover the components of the Essential Elements of the plans in detail. Each chapter starts with a brief overview, followed by a scorecard that helps you assess your current planning process. Next comes the complete set of Essential Elements that together make up that plan.

To build each of these four plans, your team needs to work through each of the Essential Elements. This planning process is straightforward, yet can require significant thought, debate, and iteration. If the team gets stalled on a particular element, it may help to momentarily put it on the shelf and go to the next element. Then come back to the skipped element once your team has had time to think more about it.

The next four chapters will cover the four plans. Chapter 2 covers the Strategic Plan, Chapter 3 covers the Business Development Plan, Chapter 4 covers the Capture Plan, and Chapter 5 covers the Proposal Plan.

Chapter 2

The Strategic Plan

The most important document for a company is its corporate Strategic Plan. It sets the stage for successful business growth by defining the vision, purpose, values, and general course direction for the entire company. Without it, the executive team cannot have a clear idea of the path they should be taking. Without this corporate blueprint, energy will be wasted as executives and managers run off to execute what they think is the best course for the company.

Another way of viewing the importance of the Strategic Plan is to consider Tony Jeary's *clarity-focus-execute* approach. In his book, *Strategic Acceleration*, Tony recommends starting with *clarity* (what you want and why), then adding *focus* (what you need to do), and finally *execution* (taking action).[viii] At the corporate level, we might view the Strategic Plan as providing clarity (vision, purpose, and value), the Business Development Plan as setting your focus, and the Capture and Proposal Plans as the execution. As one of my friends explains, not doing the corporate strategy first is like a "ready, fire, aim" approach instead of "ready, aim, fire."

The clarity-focus-execution way of thinking can also be applied individually to each of the plans. Clarity, in the Strategic Plan (Figure 2.1), refers to the defining of the values, purpose, and vision. Focus applies to the defining of the core competencies and longer-range goals. Execution applies to the shorter-range (typically, on a quarterly basis) specific goals, actions, and action plans.

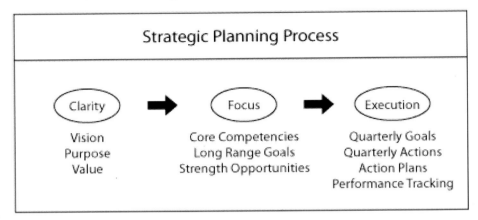

Figure 2.1 Applying Clarity-Focus-Execute to Strategic Planning

There are many excellent books on strategic planning. What is needed in today's fast-paced business environment, however, is a streamlined approach that allows the executive team to rapidly pull together their plan and then move quickly into execution.

To build your Strategic Plan, select the strategic planning team members from your executive staff. Begin by making an assessment of your current status using the Strategic Plan Scorecard.

The strategic planning process we will use (Figure 2.2) is comprised of three major steps: (1) vision and competencies, (2) strategies and analysis, and (3) quarterly goals and actions. Each of these steps contains a set of Essential Elements. Once the team has reached consensus on each of the Essential Elements, it will populate the Single-Sheet Strategic Plan template provided at the end of this chapter. This template is an excellent tool for summarizing your entire strategic plan on a single sheet of paper.

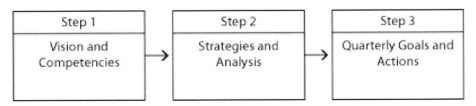

Figure 2.2 The Strategic Planning Process

At this point, you will have a great start toward defining your vision, purpose, values, core competencies, ultimate goals, one- to three-year goals, and your goals for the next quarter. You should also have a list of specific actions necessary to meet your quarterly goals.

I recommend you review your strategic plan each quarter. Start with the Strategic Plan Scorecard again, which will assist you in evaluating your current status, determining your progress, and tracking your performance. Then, repeat the planning process by stepping through the Essential Elements and updating your Single-Sheet Strategic Plan. Once the team has accomplished the initial planning, subsequent quarterly strategic planning becomes very efficient.

Strategic Planning Scorecard

Use this scorecard at the beginning of the strategic planning process to help you assess your current status. Score each question with an A (excellent), B (good), or C (not so good). When scoring, you might think about how your firm performs in each area as compared to the industry leader, or how you would envision an industry leader's performance.

Take note of any changes that have occurred this quarter or any weak areas you notice. These topics will be covered in more detail when we get to the strategic planning Essential Elements.

Table 2.1 Strategic Planning Scorecard

	Score
1. Is everyone in the company consistently using the public (branding) name or acronym?	
2. Is there agreement on clarity (mission, purpose, and value)?	
3. Has the team verified solid core competencies?	
4. Have future potential core competencies been identified?	
5. Have we thought through various strategic options?	

6. Do we have the best people in the key positions?	
7. Are we continually trying to adapt, modify, or find new best practices?	
8. Is the ultimate goal clear and concise?	
9. Is everyone in agreement that the one to three year goals are a stretch, but achievable?	
10. Has the team identified our strengths, weaknesses, opportunities, and threats (SWOT analysis)?	
11. Do we have a good understanding of our customers and their needs?	
12. Do we have knowledge of our competition's business practices and their strengths and weaknesses?	

13. Have all distractions been identified and discussed?	
14. High leverage activities (HLAs) are activities that provide us with an especially high return toward meeting our goals. Have the HLAs been identified? [This will also be covered in an Essential Element in the next section.]	
15. Do the quarterly goals support the one to three year goals and the ultimate goal?	
16. Are there specific actions defined for each quarterly goal?	
17. Will successful completion of these actions ensure that the quarterly goals will be met?	
18. Do we have a way to track the continual progress of each action?	

The Strategic Planning Essential Elements

We defined the three major steps within strategic planning as:

Step 1—vision and competencies

Step 2—strategies and analysis

Step 3—quarterly goals and actions

Each of these major steps consists of a number of Essential Elements. I'll list them here for reference, and then I'll discuss each one in depth.

Step 1—vision and competencies

- Essential Element SP-1 Company Information

- Essential Element SP-2 Vision, Purpose, Value

- Essential Element SP-3 Core Competencies

- Essential Element SP-4 Future Core Competencies

Step 2—strategies and analysis

- Essential Element SP-5 Long-Range Goals

- Essential Element SP-6 Developing Your Strategy

- Essential Element SP-7 SWOT Analysis

- Essential Element SP-8 Distractions and High Leverage Activities

Step 3—quarterly goals and actions

- Essential Element SP-9 Quarterly Goals

- Essential Element SP-10 Quarterly Actions

- Essential Element SP-11 Quarterly Action Assignments

- Essential Element SP-12 Action Plans

- Essential Element SP-13 Tracking Performance

Essential Element SP-1 Company Information

1. Legal company name:

2. Public company name or acronym:

   (Note: The public name is the name or acronym you use for your branding. It is important, for branding purposes, that the entire team—and company—be consistent in using the public name or acronym.)

3. Strategic planning team members:

4. Date for strategic plan:

5. Company slogan:

6. Company tagline (if different from slogan):

Essential Element SP-2 Vision, Purpose, Value

1. Vision:

    a. What do *we* want?

    b. Why do *we* want it?

2. Purpose:

    a. Why is our vision important to us?

3. Value:

    Why is the success of our vision important to *others?*

Essential Element SP-3 Core Competencies

There are a number of good ways to evaluate your company's core competencies. These core competencies are areas of excellence in which your firm has outstanding expertise and a demonstrative past performance. Don't be discouraged if you have difficulty quickly identifying your core competencies. This often requires significant thought and debate!

To help with the core competencies evaluation, I like to start with the four questions recommended by Bradford and Duncan in their book, *Simplified Strategic Planning*.[xii] Use a scoring system of H (high), M (medium), and L (low). The four questions to test for core competency are:

1. Is it a combination of skills, processes, and knowledge?

2. Does it differentiate the company from the competition?

3. Does it create strong value for the customer?

4. Is it difficult to copy?

Table 2.2 Core Competency Test

Candidate core competency	Test A	Test B	Test C	Test D
1.				
2.				
3.				
4.				
5.				
6.				
7.				

Essential Element SP-4 Future Core Competencies

Keep a list of potential core competencies that you may want to add at a later date. These are good to keep in mind for your next Strategic Plan review, and for consideration in your Business Development Plan.

Table 2.3 Potential Core Competencies Worksheet

Potential future core competency	Justification (Why should it be considered?)
1.	
2.	
3.	
4.	
5.	
6.	

Essential Element SP-5 Long-Range Goals

Before we begin brainstorming about specific corporate strategies, we need to agree on where we ultimately want to go. We'll need to define our ultimate, *very* long-range goal. In addition, we'll want to think out about one to three years for our long-range goals.

1. What do we consider as our ultimate business goal?

2. Where do we want to be in one to three years? [Pick a spot that's far enough to be a stretch, but not beyond reasonable expectations. Often it's good to pick one year out, three years out, or both.]

Time frame selected for goal. [Some examples of goals for service-oriented firms include revenue, number of employees, burdened rate, percent billable hours, profit, and gross earnings.]

Table 2.4 Goals Worksheet

Goals
1.
2.
3.

4.

5.

6.

7.

8.

9.

10.

Essential Element SP-6 Developing Your Strategy

In Jack Welch's book, *Winning*,[ix] he mentions that he thinks about the following three issues when developing a strategy:

1. Examine the competition, yourself, and the possibilities for the future.

2. Put the right people in the right positions.

3. Find, adapt, and continually improve your business processes.

Let's probe the first issue in depth and really analyze the competition, ourselves, and the possibilities for the future. Addressing the questions below will also help us gather information for two other strategic planning Essential Elements (competition and ourselves) that will follow. You may want to have these available as you step through these questions.

The Competition

- Who are the main customers in our industry and how do they buy?

- Who are our primary competitors?

- What are the strengths and weaknesses of each competitor?

- How good are their products and services?

- What is the market share that each competitor commands?

- What are the traits for our industry business?

- Is our business growing? How profitable is it?

- What have our competitors done differently, recently?

- What new services, products, or technologies have emerged recently?

Ourselves

- Where do we fit in the industry, and what is our market share?

- Have we changed the way we are doing things recently? Have we added or lost any key people, added or lost products or services, or won or ended significant contracts?

Possibilities for the Future

- What might our competitors do to really surprise us?

- What could we do to make our position in the market significantly stronger?

- What are our biggest risks or concerns in the near-term?

- What might we do to make our customers want to use us more than the competition?

- Are there acquisitions we should consider? What if we were to merge with another firm—would it make the two of us stronger than the sum of the parts?

Essential Element SP-7 Strengths, Weaknesses, Opportunities, and Threats (SWOT) Analysis

SWOT analysis is a great tool for helping the strategic planning team converge on a set of one to three year goals. Here, we look at the company's strengths, weaknesses, opportunities, and threats. It's best to spend the majority of time on strengths and opportunities.

Table 2.5 Strengths, Weaknesses, Opportunities, and Threats Worksheet

Our major strengths:	Our weaknesses:
Opportunities to exceed our goals:	Threats to success:

Essential Elements SP-8 Distractions and High Leverage Activities

This worksheet, in addition to the SWOT analysis, helps the team better understand and refine its understanding of the one to three year goals.

1. Distractions—are there any major distractions we need to reduce or remove to help us to be better focused on our one to three year goals?

Table 2.6 Distractions Worksheet

A.
B.
C.
D.

2. High Leverage Activities (HLAs) are activities that provide us with an especially high return toward meeting our goals. Can we focus on four to seven HLAs that would make a significant contribution toward helping us reach our one to three year goals?

Table 2.7 High Leverage Activities Worksheet

1.
2.
3.
4.
5.
6.
7.

Essential Elements SP-9 Quarterly Goals

Given our ultimate goal and our one to three year goals, we now need to determine what goals must be achieved this quarter to move us forward. In Chapter 1, I mentioned that while we were focusing in this book on strategic and business development planning, there are also several other important planning areas. The other key areas are financial planning, human relations (HR) planning, information technology (IT) planning, and operations planning. There may be other areas as well, depending upon your firm's specific structure and industry.

When deciding what goals you want to accomplish this quarter, be sure to consider all these business areas. The strategic planning team should ask the question, "What can we do this quarter to move us the fastest toward our long-range goals?"

The team will likely be able to come up with at least ten to fifteen candidate goals, spanning all of the major business areas. Now, prioritize them. Often the team will decide to keep only the top five to seven goals for the quarter, but more may be required depending upon what is needed to meet the one to three year goals. How many goals you can reasonably accomplish in a quarter depends upon the size of your company, the resources you have available, and other pressing commitments on time.

Essential Elements SP-10 Quarterly Actions

1. List the actions that are necessary to realize the quarterly goals. There should be at least one action per goal.

Table 2.8 Quarterly Goals Worksheet

Candidate actions
1.
2.
3.
4.
5.
6.
7.

8.
9.
10.
11.
12.
13.
14.
15.

2. Prioritize each action. One approach is to assign a score of A (very important), B (important), or C (less important). Once you've categorized A, B, or C, rank each action within that category. For example, if you have five A-level actions, you should end up with an A1 through A5.

Essential Elements SP-11 Quarterly Action Assignments

Assign the prioritized actions to the following table. Assign an action lead, a due date, describe the action or deliverable, and explain the measure for success.

Table 2.9 Quarterly Action Assignments

Action number	Lead	Due date	Action or deliverable item	Measure of success

Essential Element SP-12 Action Plans

Now that we've decided the actions we need to execute and have assigned action leads, we need to build Action Plans for each action. Use the following questions as a guide for building your Action Plans. The seven questions below make a good template for the sections of your Action Plan.

Table 2.10 Action Plans Worksheet

Action Plan
Action—what is the action to be completed?
Designated lead—who is the designated lead?
Deliverables—what is the precise product(s) to be delivered?
Benefits—what is the true benefit provided?

Schedule—when is this product, capability, or service absolutely needed? [Build you schedule from these dates. Include milestones for when tasks are to be completed.]

Labor and budget—what is the *approximate* labor and budget of the effort?

Labor hours:

Key individuals required:

Approximate total labor cost:

Materials and travel (cost):

Schedule or milestones:

Risks—what are the significant risks to success?

Mitigation—what should be done to mitigate these risks?

Essential Elements SP-13 Tracking Performance

Simply updating your Strategic Plan once per quarter is not enough. The executive team needs to continually track performance. It is a mistake to wait until the next quarterly update to assess your performance. At any time, you need to know the following.

- How well are we doing?
- Are we on track with our quarterly goals?
- Are we on schedule with our Action Plans?

Some (mostly larger) firms have sophisticated, real-time tracking systems for monitoring business performance. These tools can provide near real-time updates on parameters such as labor hours, costs, billable hours by client, overhead rates, general and administrative (G&A) rates, attrition, hiring, and much more.

Even if you don't have a sophisticated system in place, there are metrics you must be tracking on a regular basis. You'll need to determine the parameters to track how often each needs to be updated and who is responsible for providing the data. The goal should be to come up with a manageable set of key performance indicators with specific metrics that allow you to monitor your quarterly progress.

I'll provide some ideas, but you will need to determine what's appropriate for your industry, products and services, markets, and company. One often-used approach is to put your metrics together into a *scoreboard*, and then update the scoreboard weekly. Here are some ideas for metrics.

- *Financial metrics*—labor hours, billable hours, revenue, gross profit, return on investment (ROI), overhead rate, G&A rate, fringe rate, unallowables, travel costs, material costs, actual against planned costs

- *HR metrics*—attrition, new hires, interviews, openings, personnel actions, legal issues, trained or certified individuals, new hire in-processing and IT setup time

- *Business operations metrics*—program or project milestones, customer surveys, materials backlog

- *Business development metrics*—new awards, product sales, bids submitted, bid and proposal budget, teaming agreements

- *Relationships metrics*—how well we forge new relationships, solidify current relationships, and repair damaged relationships

- *Audit metrics*—completed audits, pass rate, action item follow-up

- *Facility maintenance and office space metrics*—facility or laboratory availability, office space planning, close-out of maintenance, supply backlog

- *IT metrics*—maintenance ticket closeout time, backlog of open maintenance tickets, uploading of new software versions, security related measures, monitoring of IT budget, tracking milestones of new IT development projects or installations

The Single-Sheet Strategic Plan

By completing all the strategic planning Essential Elements, you now have your Strategic Plan assembled. You can now consider the compiled set of Essential Elements your Strategic Plan, or you can go one step further.

After completing all the Essential Elements, I like to summarize the key points onto a single 11 × 17-inch page I call the Single-Sheet Strategic Plan. This is an especially convenient way to see everything displayed in a concise format and serves as a great quick reference tool.

The following pages show the layout of the Single-Sheet Strategic Plan. You can download this in PDF format for free at my Web site, www.trustencore.com.

Company Name

Single-Sheet Strategic Plan

Date:_____

Strategic Plan

Company Logo	

Organization Name	
Tagline	
Team Members	
Date	

VISION

What do WE want to do?

Why do WE want to do it?

CORE COMPETENCIES

1	
2	
3	
4	
5	

Ideas for future core competencies:

PURPOSE AND VALUE

What purpose will it serve?
Why is our vision important?

What value will it provide others?

LONG-TERM GOALS

Ultimate Goal:

1-3Yr Goals   *Time Period:*

1	
2	
3	
4	
5	
6	
7	

1-3YR GOALS ANALYSIS

Date To Meet for 1-3yr Goals _____ *(1-3yr out)* *Period Covered for This Quarter:* _____

Our Strengths

1	
2	
3	
4	
5	

Our Weaknesses

1	
2	
3	
4	
5	

Opportunities to exceed plan

1	
2	
3	
4	
5	

Threats to making plan

1	
2	
3	
4	
5	

Distractions to Meeting Goals

1	
2	
3	
4	
5	

High Leverage Activities (HLAs)

1	
2	
3	
4	
5	

Theme For This Period

Next Strategic Planning Session

QUARTERLY GOALS AND ACTIONS

QUARTERLY GOALS

1	
2	
3	
4	
5	

PRIORITIZED ACTIONS / ACTION PLANS FOR THIS PERIOD

Action No.	Lead	Due Date	Action / Deliverable	Measure of Success

Chapter 3

The Business Development Plan

The Business Development Plan is derived from the corporate strategy developed for the Strategic Plan. Where the Strategic Plan defines the company's overall vision and goals, the Business Development Plan charts the roadmap for the business development team's activities.

Before pursuing opportunities, you need to determine how you're going to spend your limited business development dollars, how you're going to prioritize opportunities, and how you're going to grow your customer and industry partner relationships. That's the purpose of the Business Development Plan. Like the Strategic Plan, it's an ongoing plan that must be regularly reviewed and updated.

The process of creating the Business Development Plan is relatively straightforward, with four main steps (Figure 3.1). Each step is comprised of multiple Essential Elements. These elements must be periodically updated, tweaked, scrutinized, and improved. I recommend reviewing your Business Development Plan at the same quarterly interval that you review your strategic Plan.

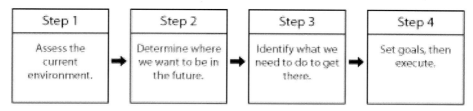

Figure 3.1 The Business development Planning Process

One particularly important component of business development is relationship building with your customers and industry partners. The practice of building and improving these relationships is called customer relationship management (CRM). If your firm has numerous sales personnel, sells a large number of products, or manages a lot of service calls, a more sophisticated commercial CRM software package is a good investment. If you are primarily a services company, then you may not need all the bells and whistles provided in these commercial CRM packages.

Nonetheless, growing your customer relationships is absolutely critical, especially in today's crowded and highly competitive services industries. A streamlined, rather than overly complex customer relationship plan is best for the services industry. I recommend that a relatively simple database solution be used. A couple of options are to use your current content management program (if it can meet all your needs) or to develop a simple database program solution.

Because of the importance of customer relationships, I have included an Essential Element relating to CRM (BP-6) in this chapter. In it, I discuss a number of related points needed for successful CRM.

Be sure to start your business development planning process by considering the questions on the Business Development Scorecard. This will help you assess the current status of your business development planning. The scorecard is followed by a detailed discussion of all of the business development Essential Elements. Carefully working through all the Essential Elements will help ensure that your Business Development Plan is comprehensive, effective, and synchronized with your Strategic Plan.

Business Development Scorecard

Use this scorecard at the beginning of the business development process to help you assess your current status. Score each question with either an A (excellent), B (good), or C (not so good). Take note of any changes that have occurred this quarter, or any weak areas you notice.

Table 3.1 Business Development Scorecard

	Score
1. Is your Business Development Plan in sync with your company's Strategic Plan?	
2. Is everyone in your company consistent with your branding, including logo and tagline?	
3. Have you defined a clear way to divide up your accounts, whether by market, customer agency, customer, or other?	
4. Does each of your account managers have a clear strategy for meeting their goals?	

5. Does your business development team have a comprehensive understanding of the business development budget? Are allocations adequate to meet your business development goals?	
6. Do you have a customer relationship process and does it work as you expect and need?	
7. Is my customer relationship system easy to use?	
8. Can I access my customer relationship while I'm on travel if need be?	
9. Can I sync my customer relationship system to my calendar, contacts, e-mails, documents, and actions?	

10. Are my customer data adequately backed up?	
11. Can I flag the decision-makers?	
12. Are we keeping track of visits and calls?	
13. Does the customer relationship system track and notify when we need to follow-up with our next call or visit?	
14. Do you have a valid means for identifying and prioritizing opportunities?	
15. Are you keeping your marketing funnel and revenue forecasts up to date?	
16. Do you have a performance measurement process in place so that you get feedback on your business development process?	

The Business Development Planning Essential Elements

We defined the four major steps within business development planning as:

    Step 1—assess the current environment

    Step 2—determine where we want to be in the future

    Step 3—identify what we need to do to get there

    Step 4—set goals and then execute them

Each of these major steps consists of a number of Essential Elements. I'll list them here for reference, and then we'll discuss each one in depth in the following pages.

Step 1—assess the current environment

- Essential Element BP-1 Market Analysis

- Essential Element BP-2 The Economy, Politics, Regulation

- Essential Element BP-3 Branding

- Essential Element BP-4 Accounts

- Essential Element BP-5 Competition

- Essential Element BP-6 Analysis of Us

- Essential Element BP-7 Customer Relations

Step 2—determine where we want to be in the future

- Essential Element BP-8 Assumptions about the Future

- Essential Element BP-9 Where We Want to Be

Step 3—identify what we need to do to get there

- Essential Element BP-10 Gap Analysis

- Essential Element BP-11 Opportunity Identification

- Essential Element BP-12 Business Development Strategies

Step 4—set goals and then execute them

- Essential Element BP-13 Prioritizing Opportunities

- Essential Element BP-14 The Sales Funnel

- Essential Element BP-15 The Business Development Budget

- Essential Element BP-16 Revenue Forecast

- Essential Element BP-17 The Business Development Schedule

- Essential Element BP-18 Goals, Actions, and Action Plans

- Essential Element BP-19 Tracking Performance

You will notice that some of the Essential Elements for the Business Development Plan are similar those in the Strategic Plan. One example is the *Analysis of Us* element. In these cases, it is important to relate the analysis to the intention of the plan. For example, the Analysis of Us for the Strategic Plan relates more to the broad corporate sense, whereas the Analysis of Us for the Business Development Plan relates more to the analysis from the viewpoint of pursuing new business opportunities.

Essential Element BP-1 Market Analysis

Understanding and defining your market is probably the most important part of building an effective Business Development Plan. There are several general questions to address:

What are your markets?

What do you offer the market?

How will your offering be unique?

How will you dominate (or be a major player) in the market?

Are you offering a commodity or a specialized product or services?

Let's look at what we need to analyze to define and better understand our market. Use Table 3.2 below as a guide.

Table 3.2 Understanding the Market Worksheet

| Market characteristics: (size, customers, methods of sale, etc) |
| Geographic considerations: |
| Customer needs: |
| Current market condition: (health of market) |

Future outlook or trends for the market: (growth rates, movement toward commodity)

Total market volume:

Our share of the total volume: (percent)

Our competitors and their share of the market:

Major customers in the market space:

Our current customers in the market space:

Essential Element BP-2 The Economy, Politics, Regulation

The economy, local and national politics, and regulation are three areas that have the potential to significantly affect your business planning. Accordingly, they should be carefully evaluated as you conduct your quarterly reviews.

Economic Outlook

Your business development team should stay current in several areas relating to the economy. These include:

- Trends in the national economy

- Trends in your state and local area

- Trends with your particular clients and industry

There are several good sources for getting this information, including periodic publications, Internet services, and specialized business opportunity providers (such as INPUT.com).[xi]

Politics

Politics can directly or indirectly have a significant effect on your business development planning. For example, in early 2010, President Obama announced that he was cancelling NASA's Constellation Program. Constellation involved hundreds of companies and over $9 billion had already been spent. A couple of months later, President Obama announced that though most of Constellation would be cancelled, pieces of it would proceed. For those firms involved in Constellation, it is critical to stay on top of the latest directions of NASA and the White House. Politics can make for very tough business planning!

Regulatory

The services and products of many industries are governed by various local, state, or federal regulations. For example, wireless industry products must operate at transmit power levels that are licensed and governed by the Federal Communications Commission (FCC). The FCC periodically changes the allowable transmit levels, so it is vital for the wireless industry to stay current with recent FCC changes.

Essential Element BP-3 Branding

The importance of branding is overlooked in many firms, but top performing firms understand the importance of presenting a consistent message, name, and logo to the customer. The importance of branding can vary from industry to industry, but nonetheless it is undoubtedly beneficial in all industries.

For industries where branding is important and warrants a sizeable budget, you may decide to engage outside expertise. When managing branding in-house, the following questions will assist you in narrowing down your approach.

1. Are we consistent with what we call ourselves? If we use an acronym for our name, are we consistent in its use?

2. Do we have a logo that reflects a positive image of what we do or represent?

3. Do we answer the phone in a consistent, friendly, and professional manner? Would it be beneficial for our customers if we had a live person answer the phone at all times?

4. Do we have a slogan or tagline that presents the message we want our clients to hear?

5. Is our Web presence professional, clean, and easy to navigate?

6. Do we have the necessary marketing material to help our BD team be successful?

7. Do we keep an up-to-date Past Performance summary as a marketing tool for our BD team for use with potential teammates?

Essential Element BP-4 Accounts

The word *accounts* can mean different things in different industries. Here, I am referring to how your firm divides up the work. For example, your company may do work for the Department of Defense (DOD) and the Department of Transportation(DOT). If so, you might have an *account lead* for the DOD business and a second *account lead* for the DOT business. Or, you may decide to have an account lead to ensure that all business with current customers is growing and have a second account lead responsible for pursuing new customers.

As you can see, there are numerous possibilities for selecting and managing your accounts. The important point is that you select a method that allows your business to grow. Depending upon the nature and size of your business, there are numerous ways to set up your accounts.

- By agency served

- By customer company

- By the individual at a customer's company

- By geographic region

- By size of business

- By type of business

- By type of contract

- By type of service provided or product line

Once you've decided how you want to divide up your business into your specific accounts, you'll need to appoint an account lead. For most small- and medium-sized businesses, it is reasonable to have a single Strategic Plan and a single Business Development Plan. But if the accounts are very large or require additional structure and process, the account lead may decide it is appropriate to develop their own Account Strategic plan or an Account Business Development Plan. This is fine as long as the Accounts Plans are aligned with the corporate plans.

Essential Element BP-5 Competition

Understanding your competition is valuable information. In some fast-paced industries, it's critical to understand where your competition is at all times. This might require quarterly, or more frequent, update of competitor information. In other slower-paced industries, monitoring the general status of the competition and providing annual updates may be sufficient. The table below provides a list of helpful information to monitor your major competitors.

Table 3.3 Competition Worksheet

Name of firm
Web site
Date of incorporation
Corporate HQ location
Core services
Executive team
Type of Business

Annual revenues
Number of employees
Core business groups
Primary clients
Core areas of expertise
Recent strategic moves (hires, transfers, acquisitions, patents)
Strengths
Weaknesses

Essential Element BP-6 Analysis of Us

In addition to understanding the competition, it is helpful to periodically step back and look into the mirror. A good corporate Strategic Plan should be doing this on a regular basis, but it is wise for the business development team to think about it as well.

The basic SWOT analysis is a good place to start. When budgeting your time, it is generally best to spend the majority of it thinking about strengths and opportunities, and less time on weaknesses and threats. Try to come up with the top five or so for each of these four areas.

Table 3.4 Strengths, Weaknesses, Opportunities, and Threats Worksheet

Our major strengths:	Our weaknesses:
Opportunities to exceed our goals:	Threats to success:

Essential Element BP-7 Customer Relationships

Customer Relationship Management is the cornerstone of many businesses. An increasing number of services firms are recognizing the importance of developing and maintaining strong relationships with their customers.

The CRM process can quickly get very complicated, so it is best to think about what you actually need before committing to a particular process or CRM tool. For this element, we will discuss several important topics relating to CRM that will assist you in making an informed decision.

CRM System Requirements

If you develop your own system, start simple and add complexity as needed. If you purchase a CRM tool, make sure it provides what you need, but that it is not overly complex.

Here are some basic requirements to consider for your customer relationship system:

- Synchronizes with your calendars, e-mail, and contacts list

- Is Web-based, so your team can access it anywhere

- Stores basic customer data such as name, address, phone number, e-mail, title

- Stores extended customer data such as personal information (family, hobbies, etc.), whether they are a decision-maker or influencer

- Able to track and log all calls, visits, documents

- Able to track and assign actions as needed

Depending on your business, a *customer* can include your clients, your industry partners, competitors, friends, subject matter experts, and more.

Identifying Key Relationships

Use this worksheet to help identify the key individuals whose relationship you want to cultivate. One method is to create two key individuals lists: one for your clients or customers and one for your potential industry partners. These lists might include individuals with the following titles:

Clients or customers:

- Program managers (PMs)

- Technical leads

- Contracting officers (CO) or leads

- Contracting officer technical representatives (COTR)

- Others

Potential industry partners:

- Company executives

- Program or project managers

- Business development

- Technical leads

- Others

Developing Relationships

Once you have a good idea about whom you want to build relationships with, you need to devise a plan for developing those relationships. Here are some considerations to build into your customer relationship plan. Use these ideas to decide how to build an action plan for developing the relationships.

1. How do I want to initially contact this individual—via another contact, an e-mail, or a cold call?
2. Can I read their bio ahead of time to get a feel for their expertise or areas of interest?
3. Should I develop a visit schedule or a call schedule?
4. Are there interesting articles or information I might send them once in a while?
5. Is there a way we might socialize, by going to lunch or a social event?

Essential Element BP-8 Assumptions about the Future

Your business development strategy is going to serve as your rudder to guide your team as you move forward. The assumptions you make about the future are key in developing this strategy. Will the economy get stronger or weaker? Will your primary customer increase or decrease their demand for you? What is the likelihood that a regulation or tax law will be passed that could significantly impact your business? These are the kinds of issues to think about when establishing the set of assumptions to guide your business development strategy.

Defining the timeframe for your assumptions is important as well. I have found that a good initial timeframe for most businesses is the next year. Depending upon your industry, and how fast things are changing, you may need to shorten the horizon or do both a short-term and far-term set of assumptions.

One approach is to think about two areas of assumptions: (1) the international and domestic climate, and (2) your particular business climate. Here are some questions to address to assist you in developing assumptions.

International and domestic business climate:

- How might the world economic situation change?

- How might the domestic business climate change?

- How might market supplies and demand change?

- How might our customer base change?

Our particular business climate:

- What might change with our customers?

- What might our competitors do?

- What things could go wrong that would significantly affect business?

Essential Element BP-9 Where We Want to Be

Similar to strategic planning, the business development team should think about where it wants to be in the future. For example, does the team want to double the number of proposals being submitted, thus increasing the marketing pipeline? If so, what are the staffing, training, tools, and budget implications?

First, decide on the appropriate horizon. If at all possible, try to synchronize the business development horizon with the timeframe used for the strategic planning goals. As for strategic planning, looking out at a one-year horizon is sufficient for many industries. But you may also want to think beyond one year, depending upon your industry.

Next create a picture of where the business development team needs to be in order to achieve these strategic goals. The following areas should be considered:

- Revenue or sales goals

- Proposal submittals

- Staffing needed

- Resources needed

- Training

- Budget (labor, travel, materials)

- IT hardware and software

- Specialized tools or services

- Outside consultants or subject matter experts

Essential Element BP-10 Gap Analysis

A gap analysis should be performed before really diving into the opportunities and business development strategies you want to pursue. Simply put, the gap is defined as the difference between our current business development and where we want to be at some point in the future. You need to analyze these gaps from a variety of perspectives and then keep these perspectives in mind as you work on business development opportunities and strategies. Use the following to analyze your gaps:

Personnel:

- Is our staff the correct size to support our growth?

- Are there strategic hires we need to consider?

Tools and services:

- Are there tools or services we need to acquire?

Budget:

- What budget do we need to reach our future goals?

Skills and Training:

- Are there particular skills we need to develop?

- Do we need any specialized training?

- Are there new core competencies that the Strategic Plan should consider in order to help the business be more competitive?

Customer relationships:

- What existing customer relationships should be improved or expanded?

- What new customer relationships do we need to develop?

- Are there new markets with new customers that need to be developed?

Industry relationships:

- What existing industry relationships should be improved or expanded?

- What new industry relationships or partnerships do we need to develop?

- Are there firms we should consider acquiring, or a merger that might be considered, that would be beneficial to both parties?

Outside consultants or subject matter experts (SMEs):

- Are there periods or specific tasks where we will need outside consultants or SMEs?

Essential Element BP-11 Opportunity Identification

In our discussion of Essential Element BD-6, we identified a few top-level opportunities to potentially pursue. Once this is done, we need to dig deeper and start identifying very specific targets.

Depending upon the type of business you do, opportunities can be of several types. You might be one of the very fortunate few where your customer sole-sources work because of your expertise. Most service companies, however, must either bid as a prime or a subcontractor to win work.

If you are bid as a subcontractor on a proposal, you must, at minimum, provide past performance and cost details. Usually, you will participate in reviewing the early proposal material and annotated outline (Pink team review) or the final proposal (Red team review). Also, you might be asked to assist with portions of the proposal preparation.

If you are bidding as the prime on a proposal, you will need to be involved in every step and activity in the capture and proposal phases. No easy task!

Whether a prime contractor or subcontractor, you need to be continually aware of potential opportunities in your industry. Keeping track of these opportunities, and finding out when new ones surface, can be daunting.

The Federal government provides a service called FedBizOpps.[x] This service is free and very useful for smaller firms. But as soon as you can afford it, you need to move to one of the commercial firms providing opportunity search services. These services are invaluable in saving both time and effort.

One of these tools, INPUT,[xi] for example, allows the user to set up searches that do a number of things. These sophisticated tools allow you to search by agency, request for proposal (RFP) release dates, size of opportunity, and many other parameters. INPUT will even notify you when a parameter on a particular opportunity changes.

Before you begin searching for opportunities, estimate the number of opportunities you need to meet your goals over the next year or two. Make a list of opportunities available using whatever market research tool you have available. You may need to tighten up the parameters so your lists aren't too long. For example, if you need to bid on fifteen opportunities over the next year, you may want to repeatedly narrow the search until you have thirty good candidates. This can then be your initial list for selecting the final fifteen.

Essential Element BP-12 Business Development Strategies

Before prioritizing these new opportunities, it's best to take some time to align them with your business development strategy. This is different from developing corporate strategies in that we are now looking at how our business development process is going to achieve our corporate goals.

Just as we did for the Strategic Plan, think about using the *clarity-focus-execute* approach. How do we clarify what we want to achieve? How do we then focus our business development path? Finally, how do we go and execute our plan?

We'll cover the plan execution when we discuss turning goals into actions and action plans. For now, let's work on our strategic and clarity and focus.

Strategic Clarity

In *Simplified Strategic Planning*, Bradford and Duncan point out that there are six areas of strategic focus.[xii] Our first step, then, is to clarify our focus area. The six areas are:

- Products and services

- Capabilities

- Markets and customers

- Technology

- Raw materials supply

- Method of sale or distribution

Even though your company may, and probably does, overlap into more than one of these six focus areas, it's generally best to select one focus area.

Strategic Focus

Once we've selected our strategic area, it's time to focus on what we need to do. We will want to address a series of issues that together will help focus our particular path.

Table 3.5 Strategic Focus Worksheet

Are there core competencies we should consider adding?
Are there skills or expertise we need that we don't currently have?
Is there sufficient demand or funding available in our markets to allow us to reach our future goals?
Are there other markets that we should consider entering?

Should we consider a merger or acquisition as a way of gaining expertise, customers, contracts, or markets?

How do we stack up against the competition with regard to cost, quality, reputation, market share, customers, capital, and staffing?

Are we a commodity or specialty, and are we where we want to be with respect to where the market is headed?

What's our competitive strategy? Are we low cost, do we offer unique products or services, or are we in a specialty niche market?

Essential Element BP-13 Prioritizing Opportunities

Prioritizing potential opportunities really consists of three steps: evaluation, rank-ordering, and deciding whether or not to pursue.

Evaluation

There are a number of factors that can be used for evaluating new opportunities. A fairly complete list is provided below, but your team may want to delete some of these or add more of its own:

- Return on investment

- Alignment with our vision and values

- Our ability to perform the work

- Customer's perception of us

- Our desire to do the work

- Resources needed

- Bid and proposal cost

- Our ability to staff the effort

- Likelihood of winning

- Our ability to support proposal preparation

- Future opportunities or benefits it might provide us

Rank-Ordering

There are several options for rank-ordering the opportunities, ranging from quantitative to qualitative. On the qualitative side, you may have enough information to quickly make a well-informed, gut estimate of the rank ordering.

More often than not, however, there is debate among the team members concerning priorities. The more quantitative, or objective, approach is to come up with a weighting based on the relative importance of each of the factors above. Then, score (or have each team member score) each opportunity against the factor and apply the weighting. This will provide a weighted score for each opportunity that you can then use to prioritize.

To Pursue or Not Pursue

Now that the opportunities are rank-ordered, it's time to decide whether or not to pursue. There are usually far more opportunities available than there is funding available for pursuit, so the team must make the difficult *Pursuit Go/No Go* decision. But the good news is that this is relatively easy because the opportunities are rank ordered. A difficulty arises, however, when another great opportunity surfaces, causing the rank-ordering to change.

The budget, schedule, and revenue Essential Elements will help the team decide where the cutoff needs to be, and thus identify the best opportunities to pursue. The Pursuit Go is then given to those top opportunities that fall within the available budget. Tweaks need to be made to the plan as new opportunities surface or as quarterly or annual business development planning is conducted.

Essential Element BP-14 The Sales Funnel

There are many formats for Sales Funnels. The important point is to create one that allows you to track and prioritize both your current business and your new business opportunities.

Often, each account lead or group lead will build their own funnel, which will later be consolidated at the corporate level. Some firms, with centralized business development teams, will keep just one consolidated funnel at the corporate level.

It is usually best to start simple and then add complexity as needed. I recommend starting with the following major categories for opportunities:

- Current contracts (efforts under contract)

- High potential (bids submitted or high likelihood of winning the work in next thirty days)

- Medium potential (Pursuit Go has been given, likely to get work in next quarter)

- Watch (promising opportunities to watch, research, or grow over next six months)

Under each category, at a minimum, you will want to track the following: opportunity name, description, BD team lead, significance, size, location of work to be performed, customer name and agency, significant dates, last action, and next action.

Essential Element BP-15 The Business Development Budget

The strategic planning process will produce a budget for business development. It is then the responsibility of the business development team to make the best use of that budget in its allocation process.

The allocation process will, by necessity, be iterative. Knowing the size of the business development team, one can create an initial budget by just running out labor, travel, and materials costs for the next four quarters. If the team is going to pursue more opportunities next year and the budget is bigger, then decide how to allocate the additional funds (hiring new staff, more travel, or additional purchases).

This initial budget cut will need to be revised (usually a umber of times) once the revenue forecast and the business development schedule are developed. These revisions provide additional information on how many new opportunities to pursue.

As part of the business development process, the team will decide how much effort will be required for each new pursuit. Again, this is an iterative process that will become smoother each quarter once the process is established.

Getting back to budget planning, here are a few high-level items to initially consider:

- Business development team labor

- Subject matter experts/consultants labor

- Travel

- Conference fees

- Materials

Essential Element BP-16 The Revenue Forecast

Once you've identified opportunities, evaluated them, and prioritized them in your marketing funnel, then you are ready to build a revenue forecast. The revenue, or sales, forecast is often built by the BD team, but coordinated closely with the CFO.

The purpose of the revenue forecast is to accurately estimate your future revenues. It basically takes the win probability, size, and duration information for each opportunity and time-phases this over a two to three year period. When you add the figures up for all the opportunities, you get the estimated revenue over time.

The revenue forecast is a vital tool that serves multiple roles. It allows the BD team to see the big picture. It allows the HR team to plan for upsizing or potential downsizing. It further allows the CFO to predict revenues, thereby aiding cash-flow planning.

Let's discuss a simple template for developing a revenue forecast. The top block of the template would contain a row for each of your current contracts. The rows across would be, at a minimum:

- Contract manager of lead

- Total value of contract

- Start date

- Stop date

- Win odds (100 percent for a current contract)

- Expected revenue by quarter (or month)

Below the current contract block, you would create three additional blocks are for your opportunities. These are opportunities you plan to bid (ones that you've already decided to pursue). The three blocks should be titled:

- Submitted proposals

- Planned proposals

- Watch opportunities

The submitted proposals block contains opportunities where you've already submitted the bid and where you likely have a good feel for the odds of winning. The planned proposals are the proposals you plan to pursue over the next year. The win odds for these are likely more uncertain. Finally, the third block is just a list of any promising opportunities you may be watching. The win odds for these should be kept at 0 percent until the decision to move them into the planned proposals group.

By the way, a good sanity check is to see what your average win rate is for all your opportunities. If it's much higher than your historical win rates, then your revenue forecast is likely too optimistic. If it's much lower, then you may be too pessimistic in your forecast.

Essential Element BP-17 The Business Development Schedule

The business development schedule is very important for a number of reasons. Business development teams have limited time availability, personnel, travel budgets, and materials. The schedule is the means for efficiently synchronizing these limitations together.

Your revenue forecast provides the team with approximately how many new opportunities are needed. Knowing or making an informed guess at your win-rate will tell you how many opportunities you will need to pursue.

Next, you will need to take the budget you have available and spread it across the opportunities you need to pursue. Likewise, you need to allocate your available personnel and outside expertise needed across these pursuits.

Now you need to ask some tough questions:

- Does our team have the budget it needs?

- If not, can we get more funding to pursue certain opportunities?

- Are we getting the win-rate we expect? Can we do better?

- Are the personnel and resources available when we need them?

- Are there other key personnel or experts we should bring on board?

- Are there contingencies in place for the more likely unexpected events?

- Are we staying in sync with the revenue forecast and the Strategic Plan?

Because it's common for these potential opportunities to change in scope, schedule, go away, or for new opportunities to surface, the schedule must be monitored to keep things running smoothly.

Essential Element BP-18 Goals, Actions, and Action Plans

Similar to what was accomplished for the Strategic Plan, we now want to develop our business development goals, actions, and action plans. Depending upon the size of the company and the pace of operations, the team may want to set quarterly or annual business development goals. As with the Strategic Plan, each goal should have at least one action and designated lead identified. Finally, an action plan should be developed for each action.

Goals

Annual goals may be enough for some firms, but most will want to have quarterly goals. These goals should be derived from the firm's Strategic Plan goals.

Actions

These should be one or more actions for each business development goal. These actions define how the team intends to achieve the goal.

Action Plan Issues

There are a number of issues that should be resolved prior to building the detailed action plans. These include the following:

Who is the designated lead?

What is the precise product to be delivered?

What is the true benefit provided?

Is there a date by which this product, capability, or service is absolutely needed?

What is the approximate (very high-level at this point!) scope of the effort in time, money, and resources?

- Labor hours:

- Key individuals required:

- Approximate labor cost:

- Materials and travel required (cost):

- Schedule (calendar time):

What are the significant risks to success? What should be done to mitigate these risks?

Action Plans

Action plans should be developed using the same format as described for action plans in the Strategic Plan. Refer to Essential Element SP-12.

Essential Element BP-19 Tracking Performance

The BD team should track certain measures, or metrics, to ensure they are consistent with the BD budget, in sync with the company's strategic plan, and provide a continual feedback mechanism.

There are many ways to implement a performance measures process. The best solution will be dependent upon several factors, including the size of the company, the structure and complexity of the company, and the types of measures that need to be tracked.

The process can be as simple as someone regularly entering data into a spreadsheet, or as complex as a Web-based database serving the entire company in multiple locations.

The BD team should track several basic measures, which often include:

- BD expenditures by category (labor, travel, materials, conferences or meetings, etc.)

- Funds spent for each proposal

- Number of proposals given Pursuit Go

- Number of proposals given Bid Go

- Number of proposals submitted

- Win rates for proposals, possibly by agency

Chapter 4

The Capture Plan

Capturing is positioning yourself to win. Most customers nowadays are looking for a collaborative partner relationship rather than simply another vendor or supplier. So, the Capture Plan is all about building a collaborative relationship, developing a value-based solution, and distinguishing yourself in your customers' eyes from your competition.

Let's start with defining the basic components of a Capture Plan, and then we'll go into the details of the Essential Elements involved in building a solid Capture Plan.

A Capture Plan can be boiled down to six basic components or steps (Figure 4.1). They are:

1. The opportunity

2. The capture team, budget and schedule

3. The customer

4. The competition

5. Analysis of us

6. Our strategy and approach

Figure 4.1 The Capture Planning Process

Competition for new business is so fierce that it's not unusual for the capture planning to begin two to five years prior to the RFP release. The information that will be collected in the capture phase will be invaluable in the proposal phase. The Essential Elements that make up these six components will ensure that you will be capturing the right information. Let's start with our Capture Plan Scorecard and then move right into the Essential Elements.

Capture Plan Scorecard

Use this scorecard at the beginning of the capture planning process to help assess your current status. Score each question with either an A (excellent), B (good), or C (not so good).

Table 4.1 Capture Plan Scorecard

	Score
1. Do we completely understand the opportunity? What are our gaps in understanding?	
2. Are our capture team assignments made, and does everyone understand their roles and responsibilities?	
3. Can we meet the budget and schedule?	
4. Do we have the customer relationships we need, or can we build them in time?	
5. Do we have a solid understanding of the customers' needs and concerns?	
6. What risks are associated with this opportunity?	

7. Do we understand the competition well enough?	
8. Do we have a plan for exploiting our strengths and mitigating our weaknesses?	
9. What distinguishes us and our approach from our competitors?	
10. Have we developed powerful strategies for this bid?	
11. Do we have a number of innovations to include?	
12. What positioning do we need to do to help ensure a win?	
13. Do our teammates fill weaknesses or add necessary strengths?	
14. Have we considered a contingency strategy for what might go wrong during the capture and proposal plans?	

The Capture Planning Essential Elements

We defined the six major steps within business development planning as:

> Step 1—the opportunity
>
> Step 2—the capture team, budget, schedule
>
> Step 3—the customer
>
> Step 4—the competition
>
> Step 5—analysis of us
>
> Step 6—our strategy and approach

Each of these major steps consists of a number of Essential Elements. I'll list them here for reference, and then we'll discuss each one in depth in the following pages.

Step 1—the opportunity:

- Essential Element CP-1 The Opportunity

Step 2—the capture team, budget, schedule:

- Essential Element CP-2 The Capture Team

- Essential Element CP-3 Budget

- Essential Element CP-4 Schedule

Step 3—the customer:

- Essential Element CP-5 Customer Analysis

- Essential Element CP-6 Needs or Concerns

- Essential Element CP-7 Visits and Supporting Material

Step 4—the competition:

- Essential Element CP-8 Competition Analysis

Step 5—analysis of us:

- Essential Element CP-9 Analysis of Us

Step 6—our Strategy and approach:

- Essential Element CP-10 Key Win Strategies and Positioning

- Essential Element CP-11 Key Managers, Key Personnel, and Initial Organizational Chart

- Essential Element CP-12 Distinguishers, Innovations, and Enhancements

- Essential Element CP-13 Teammate Selection

- Essential Element CP-14 Subject Matter Experts

- Essential Element CP-15 Past Performance

- Essential Element CP-16 NDAs and Teaming Agreements

- Essential Element CP-17 IT Support

- Essential Element CP-18 Cost Analysis and ROI

Essential Element CP-1 The Opportunity

A basic set of information needs to be gathered for each opportunity. Much of this information would have been considered in making the Pursuit Go decision. Start with the set provided, and add to this information as needed:

Customer office, department, branch:

Agency:

Customer contact details (decision maker and influencer names, phone numbers):

Key dates:

Total budget and annual budget:

Type contract:

Small business percentage and type:

Period of performance:

Location(s) of performance:

Incumbent(s):

Potential risks (funding, technical, schedule):

Essential Element CP-2 Team Assignments

The capture team is often significantly smaller than the proposal team. On smaller efforts, capture team individuals may need to double-up on certain roles. Below is the minimal set of roles for the capture phase:

Capture team:

- Capture manager:

- Cost analyst:

- Technical (or mission) lead:

- Text and graphics lead:

- IT lead:

Proposal team

Proposal manager

Some capture phases can start one or more years prior to RFP release. Thus, there may be significant time for the proposal manager to make assignments and to get the various proposal leads to establish their teams. The proposal leads and proposal manager should also work with the capture team in ensuring they get the information they need well ahead of the start of the proposal phase.

Essential Element CP-3 Budget

The Business Development Plan should establish the budget available for the capture and proposal phases. It is the responsibility of the capture manager, however, to carefully plan and review the allocated budget to ensure it provides the funds to produce a winning proposal.

Like most budgets, this will be a somewhat iterative process. As a first cut, the capture manager, often working with the proposal manager, should make a simple estimate of how to allocate the funds between the capture and proposal phases. This will primarily consist of making estimates of the labor, travel, and materials needed in each phase.

Capture team cost estimate:

- Capture team labor:

- Subject matter experts/consultants labor:

- Travel:

- Materials:

- Other costs:

Proposal team cost estimate:

- Proposal team labor:

- Subject matter experts/consultants labor:

- Travel:

- Materials:

- Other costs:

Total cost estimate:

- Capture phase subtotal:

- Proposal phase subtotal:

- Grand total:

Essential Element CP-4 Schedule

The capture phase can sometimes extend for quite a long time. On very large services bids, for example, the capture phase can start several years prior to the RFP release.

In addition to understanding the opportunity and pulling together the team and budget, you need to decide exactly what the team needs to accomplish in the time available. This will include at least the following:

- Gathering information ultimately used in the proposal phase

- Strengthening your relationship with the customer

- Gaining a better understanding of the competition

- Staying current on any potential scope or funding changes in the opportunity

- Positioning your firm to win

- Developing winning strategies

- Deciding the best partners (teammates) for the bid

We'll cover these topics in more detail in some of the following Essential Elements discussions. With respect to the schedule, though, you will need to decide exactly how the capture team is going to address all these issues. For example, you might decide that "strengthening your relationship with the customer" will involve multiple informal visits to the customer and attendance at several formal gatherings (such as an industry day or formal site tour).

First, lay out a schedule. Be prepared to iterate on the schedule as you work through the other capture planning Essential Elements. Also, be sure to continue to verify that all elements of the schedule can be covered by the allotted capture budget.

Essential Element CP-5 Customer Analysis

During the capture phase, the capture team will need to gather as much information as possible about the customer. Prior to each phone call or visit, a list of specific questions or topics should be defined so that the limited time with the customer is optimized.

In addition to building or strengthening the relationship with the customer, the capture team will need to gather information critical in the success of the proposal.

- Does the customer know our strengths, past performance, and key personnel?

- What do they think of us?

- Who are the key individuals and what are their roles?

- Are there any customer personnel changes that may occur prior to the award?

- What strong relationships does the customer have, and how do we fit in? Do they appear to have favorite firms or individuals?

- What does the customer see as their biggest concern areas or upcoming challenges?

- Does the customer have any thoughts on ideas for innovations or improvements?

- What can be done better?

- What is the strength of the program and funding? What is the future funding profile and is it likely to change?

- What distractions does the customer have? Is there anything that the contractor might do to help alleviate these distractions?

- Does the customer have any feedback on rates or cost, or concerns in this area? How important are rates and cost for this effort?

- How important is past performance? How important are certain core competencies?

- Can we gather any feedback on the incumbent team? How motivated are the current employees?

Essential Element CP-6 Customer Needs and Concerns

Let's delve a little deeper into the specific areas of customer needs and concerns. These are critical areas to understand, as they provide especially fertile material for the proposal phase.

Needs

The RFP will contain very detailed descriptions of the formal requirements for the opportunity. However, the capture phase offers us a unique opportunity to both gather advance intelligence on what the requirements will likely be, as well as influence the final RFP requirements to our benefit.

Specific information on needs can be gathered from a number of sources. If the contract is a rebid of an existing contract, the requirements from the current contract is a good place to start. Even with a rebid, however, significant changes to the requirements are likely to occur. Hopefully, the extent of these changes can be determined through meetings with the customer in advance of the RFP release.

For new bids, direct meetings with the customer contracting, programmatic, and technical leads are a must. Also, stronger relationships with the customer are directly proportional to the details of the information you're able to get.

Concerns

Gaining a deep understanding of your customer's concerns can be vital in producing a winning proposal. The stronger your relationship with the customer, the higher the likelihood that he or she will be comfortable enough to really share what they'd like to see addressed in the proposal. The RFP requirements will spell out most of what the customer wants, but there are always underlying concerns that, for some reason or another, did not make it into the RFP. To really root out these concerns, you will likely need to have one-on-one meetings with key contracts, programmatic, and technical leads from the customer side. If addressed properly, these concerns can turn into distinguishers or innovations that make your proposal stand out from the competition.

Essential Element CP-7 Customer Visits and Supporting Material

Customer visits are important for both building relationships and for gathering critical proposal information. Let's discuss three related aspects: customer visits, site visits, and supporting material.

Customer Visits

At the very beginning of the capture phase, the capture manager needs to make an initial guess of which customers to visit. To make the most of these visits, carefully write out the purpose for the visit, who is to be visited, and exactly what needs to be asked to each customer visited. Following the visit, a *call log* should be completed that summarized who was visited and what transpired. The types of customers to visit can vary significantly depending upon the type of opportunity, but here are a few ideas:

- Contracting officers or leads

- Technical leads

- Program managers

- Other individuals that may interface with the contract

- Users of products or services from the contract

Site Visits

Site visits are typically accomplished for the purpose of checking out labs, hardware, facilities, or for watching operations. While the focus of these are typically not to visit customers, many times a customer visit can, and should, be integrated into a site visit. At the beginning of the capture phase, the team should determine which sites need to be visited prior to RFP release.

Supporting Material

Supporting material is information that the team might provide to the customer (usually to influence the RFP) or information that the team needs from the customer. The capture team should determine what material they need to provide or acquire early in the process.

For example, the capture manager might decide to put together a white paper that discusses the advantages to the customer of adding certain requirements to the RFP. This white paper would then be provided to the customer in hopes of influencing the wording of the RFP.

On the other side, the capture manager might request that the customer provide the capture team with certain documents relating to the upcoming opportunity. Much of the time, the customer will either release the material directly to the team or will set up an electronic library where all bidders will then have online access to this material.

Essential Elements CP-8 Competition Analysis

Gaining an understanding of the competition can provide valuable insight in refining strategies for your proposal. You can look for weaknesses to exploit, or ways to counter their claims of strength. The questions to address are fairly straightforward:

Competitor name:

Likely teammates:

Strengths:

> What are their strengths with respect to this opportunity?
>
> What might we do or offer to counter these strengths

Weaknesses:

> What are their weaknesses with this opportunity?
>
> How can we exploit these weaknesses?

Essential Elements CP-9 Analysis of Us

In addition to analyzing the competition, it's important to gain an objective understanding of your particular strengths and weaknesses. For this analysis, be sure to ask for perspectives that are outside of your immediate team.

Our likely teammates:

Strengths:

> What are our strengths with respect to this opportunity?
>
> What are our teammates' strengths with respect to this opportunity?
>
> What might we do to emphasize our strengths for this opportunity?

Weaknesses:

> What are our weaknesses with respect to this opportunity?
>
> What are our teammates' weaknesses with respect to this opportunity?
>
> How can we minimize these weaknesses?
>
> How do we think our competitors might try to maximize these weaknesses?

Essential Elements CP-10 Key Win Strategies and Positioning

One of the more challenging components of the capture and proposal phases is developing the win strategy and then positioning the team to optimize that strategy. Understanding the customer, the competition, and yourself is a significant piece of this strategy. Customer understanding is enhanced through the site visits. Your teammates, especially if one of them is a current incumbent, will provide good intelligence.

Win Strategies

Strategies might be related to practically any area of the opportunity. These areas include cost, management approach, technical approach, key personnel, relationship-building, site visits, or the submittal of white papers. During the capture phase, significant thought should be given to formulating win strategies:

- What message or theme(s) do we want the customer to get from reading the proposal?

- What distinguishes our team from the competition?

- What innovations might we offer?

- What enhancements, beyond the scope of the contract, might we offer?

- What are some of the ways to beat the competition? What weaknesses might we allude to in the proposal?

- What are ways we might minimize the weaknesses we have that our competition will point out?

- How can we improve the perception of our team in the eyes of the customer?

- How might we highlight certain strengths or past performance of our team?

- Can we improve our relationship with the customer during the capture phase?

Positioning

Once the strategies begin to come together, it's time to start thinking about how to position the team to realize these strategies. For each of your strategies, take stock of where you currently are and then decide where you'd like to be when the proposal is submitted. Then figure out what the team needs to do to get there.

Essential Elements CP-11 Key Managers, Key Personnel, and Initial Organizational Chart

Early on in the capture phase, the capture manager should begin putting together three things relating to key individuals. The first, and most important, are the key individuals who will be leading and managing the new opportunity. The second are any other key personnel, such as technical or specialty area leads. The third is an early cut at an organizational chart. As you meet with the customer during the capture phase, ask for any thoughts they have about filling key roles or how they think an organizational chart should be structured.

Key Managers

Key managers might consist of one to two personnel for a small contract, or up to a dozen or more for a big bid. These are folks that you plan to propose in critical roles, including the general manager, department directors, program or project managers, the HR lead, and the IT lead. It's almost always better to name these folks explicitly in the proposal, rather than saying something like "we'll tell you who it will be if you award us the contract."

Key Personnel

In addition to the key managers, there may be other individuals whose explicit mentioning by name in the proposal will help the odds of winning. These might include positions such as senior technical folks, the safety officer, the security officer, or the facilities manager.

Organizational Chart

An in-depth organizational chart will almost undoubtedly be required for the proposal. A fairly detailed organizational chart should be ready to go by the time the proposal phase kicks off.

Essential Element CP-12 Distinguishers, Innovations, and Enhancements

Simply addressing the basic requirements of the RFP will almost certainly not be enough to win the bid. There are three additional things in a winning proposal: distinguishers, innovations, and enhancements. The approach for these is best worked out during the capture phase. Be careful not to smother the proposal with these, but try to determine the appropriate balance for the customer and RFP.

Distinguishers

Distinguishers are areas in which you offer an advantage over your competition. You will want to highlight these in your proposal. These might be areas such as your especially low rate structure, some special core competency, the key personnel you are proposing, an innovative approach, or excellent past performance on a related contract.

Innovations

Innovations are *out-of-the-box* approaches that you offer for meeting RFP requirements. For example, you might offer a cost-saving, online means for employees who are at remote sites or are travelling to do their timecards. Or, you might leverage a particular business tool that is used on one of your other contracts.

Enhancements

Enhancements are added features that add value to the contract, but that were not explicitly mentioned in the RFP requirements. The question, however, is, "Who pays for it?" Offering enhancements can, in the customers' eyes, be viewed as tremendously helpful, as something they find unbeneficial, or somewhere in-between. Paying for enhancements is the tricky part. The options include paying for them out of the profits, including the enhancement as part of your regular duties, asking the customer to pay for them if they want them, offering some sort of *cost-share* approach, or including them as options on the contract. If you come up with a few clever enhancements, the customer may appreciate the initiative taken even if they decide not to implement the enhancement after all.

One challenge for the capture and proposal teams is where to incorporate distinguishers, innovations, or enhancement. One method that works well is to start with three categories relating to each of the three typical volumes of a proposal. These are the management approach, technical (or equivalent, if the proposal is not tech-heavy), and cost. Then, throughout the capture phase, keep a running list of ideas for these three categories. The meetings with the customer often provide valuable insights.

Essential Elements CP-13 Teammate Selection

In many opportunities, a prime contractor will need to bring in teammates. It might be that the contract requires that a certain percentage of the revenues go to small business. It could be that the prime doesn't have all the core competencies necessary to cover the RFP requirements. Or, it could be that the teammate brings a close relationship with the customer or exemplary past performance. Either way, the addition of a teammate should make the overall team stronger in some manner.

Formal team selection (signing a legally binding Teaming Agreement) of the team can occur at any time, but often the prime will wait until the final version of the RFP is released. It may be that the prime will want to lock in commitments prior to final RFP release, but there is some risk in this approach for everyone because no one can be sure of what's in the RFP until it is formally released.

Selecting a teammate is serious business. Select the wrong one, and you could do serious harm to your reputation, past performance, or your bottom line. As you are considering teaming with someone else as a subcontractor or the prime, address the following questions:

- Do they have a good reputation with the customer?

- Do their core competencies add value for this effort?

- Do they have excellent past performance?

- Is their cost within the bounds of what we need to propose?

- Are they financially sound?

- Can they perform as needed on this contract?

- Do they have the personnel with the necessary skills available at the time needed, or can they get them?

- Are their contracting, finance, and HR departments adequate?

- Are there any cultural or values-related issues that might be an impediment?

Essential Elements CP-14 Subject Matter Experts

To help reduce costs, firms want to keep their internal business development teams as small as possible. This means that the capture and proposal teams may need outside advice or assistance across a wide variety of subject matter. These advisors are usually known as subject matter experts (SMEs).

Internal SMEs

In most cases, the use of SMEs within your own firm is the most cost effective. SMEs within your firm can sometimes do a little bit of work on their own time, especially if they have a vested interest or desire in helping their company succeed. If their time does need to be reimbursed, which is often the case, the capture and proposal managers must be sure to include these labor costs in their budget.

External SMEs

Often, your company either will not have the internal expertise needed, or the individuals with the requisite expertise will not be available when you need them. Thus, external SMEs must be secured well in advance, often using consulting agreements.

Whether internal or external SMEs are needed, try to identify the extent of the support needed early in the capture phase. This will allow the SMEs to be available when needed and for them to be properly accounted for in the budget.

Essential Elements CP-15 Past Performance

RFPs will often ask for past performance information in a specific format, or they will ask for specific information relating to that exact bid. However, it's always a good idea to have a generic paper listing your firm's past performance on hand. This not only makes it quicker to build the specific past performance write-ups, but it is a great tool for discussions with potential teammates during the capture phase.

Past performance write-ups vary from being very brief to very lengthy, the length being largely determined by what is expected in your industry. There are a number of ways to structure past performance write-ups. Perhaps the most common is to base the structure on your firm's core competencies. This works very well if your firm has very specific core competencies.

Another approach is to base the structure upon the customers or agencies your firm supports. This works very well for firms that have less-specific competencies, such as one that might provide "general engineering and technical services."

Essential Elements CP-16 NDAs and Teaming Agreements

Nondisclosure agreements (NDAs) and teaming agreements (TAs) are two legal documents that are needed throughout the strategic and business development processes. It's helpful to review the purpose of these documents and to understand when they are needed.

Nondisclosure Agreements

NDAs are used in the capture phase to protect (keep private) the intellectual property of the firms involved. For example, a prime might decide that it needs to team with a single *8a* (disadvantaged) small business. During the course of the capture phase, however, the prime might want to share or get information from two 8a firms before making a decision. The prime will then sign an NDA with each of these 8a firms so that confidential discussion can be held and information discreetly shared.

Teaming Agreements

Teaming agreements are used once the final teammates have been selected. This usually occurs early in the proposal phase, immediately after the formal RFP is released. The TA is the legal agreement between the prime contractor and each subcontractor. This agreement will vary based on the type of arrangement needed for the effort, or it can be based on the business practices that the prime wants to contract (such as using a consolidated timekeeping system or intertwined financial reporting system). One of the important issues the TA addresses is what percent of revenues or type of work the subcontractor is expected to receive from the contract. For example, if the customer levies a 3 percent veteran-owned small business requirement in the RFP, then the TA might specify that Company A (a veteran-owned small business) will receive an annual average of 3 percent of contract revenues.

Essential Elements CP-17 IT Support

Reliable IT support and document control is especially important during the capture and proposal phases. Files should be carefully dated, stored electronically, and routinely backed up. If a file becomes corrupted, the team should be able to revert back to the most recent version easily. Horror stories abound of capture or proposal teams that have lost crucial data and are not able to recover it prior to the proposal due date. There is no excuse for this happening with the IT tools available today. Here are a few of the main IT-related issues to consider:

- What will we use as our document repository system?

- How will we provide configuration control for our electronic files and media?

- What computers and peripherals does the team need?

- Any special cell phone or audio-visual needs?

- What specialty software does the team need?

   o   Word processing:

   o   Graphics and design:

   o   Presentation:

   o   Other:

- How will we provide Internet access and ensure IT security?

- Will we do the final proposal printing and media preparation internally or will we outsource it?

Essential Elements CP-18 Cost Analysis and ROI

Contracts can come in many forms, including firm-fixed price, cost plus award fee, incentives-based, and multi-award, just to name a few. Each of these forms has important subtleties in the way that costs are calculated and profit is determined.

If you don't have good cost analysis tools and you are bidding as a subcontractor, you may be able to rely on the prime to assist you with preparing your inputs to the cost volume and in understanding some of the intricacies of the cost analysis. If you are bidding as the prime, then you really need to know what you are getting into and get expert advice if needed. Profit margins on bids, especially on government bids, have shrunk over the last decade. So a tiny mistake in your cost analysis could have a big impact on whether or not the opportunity is profitable.

In addition to a solid cost analysis tool, the business development team and the firm's CFO need to agree on what constitutes a good return on investment (ROI) for an opportunity. It is unwise to simply look at the profit proposed on a contract, and assume that because there's a percentage of profit being proposed, the ROI will be acceptable. A better means is to really dig in and look at how this effort would impact the firm's financials. For example, one might look at how this effort will impact the firm's EBITDA (earnings before interest, taxes, depreciation and amortization) have been subtracted, which is a better indicator of a company's profitability).

Chapter 5

The Proposal Plan

The proposal phase often officially kicks off when the draft RFP is released by the customer. We'll talk about the Bid Go/No Go process when we cover the Essential Elements, but you should not bid the opportunity if it's not aligned with your corporate strategy, if you haven't been executing a Capture Plan, or if you don't have the budget and resources to put together a winning proposal.

The Proposal Plan (PP), led by the proposal manager, should be as complete as possible by the time the draft RFP is released. The information gathered (well ahead of the draft RFP release!) for the Capture Plan will now be heavily relied upon to successfully execute the PP.

The draft RFP is generally expected to be a close fit to the final RFP (assuming the customer chooses to release a draft RFP, which many do). Thus, once the draft RFP comes out, The proposal manager, along with the capture manager and BD team, should do a quick assessment and determine if the RFP is along the lines of what they expected and whether they should continue to bid. The later this Bid Go/No Go decision is made, the more costly it can be to your BD budget should you decide to no go. This explains the critical importance of all the work done during the capture phase and how this information greatly aids in the ability to quickly make an informed Bid Go/No Go decision.

At the time of the draft RFP release, the proposal manager should already have a fairly good handle on many of the Essential Elements of the PP. These include the proposal team members, the budget, the schedule, a good idea of the teammates needed, subject matter experts lined up, key personnel to be proposed, and a rough outline of the proposal. The other elements will need to be quickly assembled according to the PP schedule.

I have categorized the proposal planning Essential Elements into four major steps (Figure 5.1). These steps are:

Step 1—initial setup and compliance

Step 2—teaming and personnel

Step 3—content preparation

Step 4—production and delivery

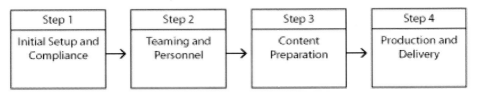

Figure 5.1 The Proposal Planning Process

The PP Essential Elements outlined in this chapter will guide your proposal team in pulling together the necessary information and process for a winning proposal. Depending upon your industry, however, you will find other elements to add. Continually improving your process is important and perhaps even critical to survival.

Proposal Plan Scorecard

Use this scorecard at the beginning of the proposal planning process to help assess your current status. Score each question with either an A (excellent), B (good), or C (not so good).

Table 5.1 Proposal Plan Scorecard

Proposal Plan Scorecard Questions	Score
1. Has the proposal team member been selected? Does everyone know their roles and do they have the time available to meet their responsibilities?	
2. Has the proposal manager stepped through the Bid Go/No Go issues, and has a Bid Go/No Go recommendation been made?	
3. Can the proposal team produce a winning proposal given the budget and schedule? Are all the necessary resources available?	
4. Has a compliance matrix been built? Are the risks understood for any simplification that was made to the compliance matrix?	
5. Have teammates been selected? Do the teammates make the team stronger in some tangible way? Are NDAs and teaming agreements in place?	

6. Have key personnel been identified for the critical contract positions?	
7. Are SMEs lined up to help where needed? Is their estimated time in the budget?	
8. Are the volume leads prepared to create an annotated outline? Has the production team defined the style sheets, layouts, and any other documents?	
9. Do the volume leads have writers lined up? Is there a writing guide that sets expectations for the quality of writing?	
10. Is the production team prepared to do layout, editing, integration, and check for flow? Are individuals assigned for final assembly, print, and delivery?	

The Proposal Planning Essential Elements

We defined the six major steps within business development planning as:

Step 1—initial setup and compliance

Step 2—teaming and personnel

Step 3—content preparation

Step 4—production and delivery

Each of these major steps consists of a number of Essential Elements. I'll list them here for reference, and then we'll discuss each one in depth in the following pages.

Step 1—initial setup and compliance

- Essential Element PP-1 The Proposal Team

- Essential Element PP-2 Bid Go/No Go

- Essential Element PP-3 The Proposal Budget

- Essential Element PP-4 The Proposal Schedule

- Essential Element PP-5 The Compliance Matrix

Step 2—teaming and personnel

- Essential Element PP-6 Teammate Selection

- Essential Element PP-7 Key Personnel

- Essential Element PP-8 Subject Matter Experts

Step 3—content preparation

- Essential Element PP-9 The Annotated Outline

- Essential Element PP-10 Proposal Writing

Step 4—production and delivery

- Essential Element PP-11 Layout

- Essential Element PP-12 Editing and Flow

- Essential Element PP-13 Integration and Page Count
- Essential Element PP-14 Final Assembly and Print
- Essential Element PP-15 Delivery
- Essential Element PP-16 Best and Final Offer

Essential Element PP-1 Proposal Team

The size of the proposal team will vary significantly based on the size and scope of the proposal. Generally, this team can be divided into five areas: the proposal manager, volume leads and writers, proposal support, reviewers, and production.

The proposal manager is ultimately responsible for the creation of a winning proposal. He or she will have worked closely with the capture manager during the capture phase and will have much of the strategy and information ready for the proposal team.

Typical proposals will consist of management, technical, and cost volumes. Often there are other volumes such as small business utilization and past performance. Each volume should have a designated lead who determines what expertise and support is needed to create the volume.

Proposal support consists of any support personnel needed by the proposal manager, including IT, contracting, subject matter experts, and administrative.

Reviewers are the personnel that lead and support the Pink, Red, and Gold team reviews.

Finally, the production team consists of personnel that do layout, graphics, editing, and media.

The following can be used as a guide for the proposal manager in assigning proposal team members. For smaller efforts, personnel might wear "two-hats."

Proposal Team Assignments

Below is an example of the typical types of personnel (or expertise) that will be needed for the proposal team:

Proposal manager:

Volume leads and writers:

- Management volume lead

- Management volume writer(s)

- Technical volume lead

- Technical volume writer(s)

- Cost volume lead

- Cost volume writer(s)/analyst(s)

- Volume lead
- Volume writer(s)
- Volume lead
- Volume writer(s)

Proposal support:
- IT services lead
- Contracts lead
- Admin support

Subject matter experts:
- SME(s)/Area(s)

Reviewers:
- Pink team lead
- Pink team member(s)
- Red team lead
- Red team member(s)
- Gold team lead
- Gold team member(s)

Production:
- Production lead
- Graphics
- Editing
- Layout
- Final preparation (printing, electronic media, electronic submittal)
- Delivery

Essential Element PP-2 Bid Go/No Go

In the process of pursuing a new opportunity there are two Go/No Go decision milestones. The first, the Pursuit Go/No Go, is made as part of your Business Development Plan. The Pursuit Go decision authorizes the capture and proposal planning. Once the capture phase begins, the team may also decide at any time to No Go the opportunity if it becomes clear that it's not winnable or not aligned with strategy.

The second Go/No Go decision is the Bid Go/No Go. This decision is generally made when the details of the RFP are released (generally, the draft RFP). Again, the team may at any time change their mind and No Go the opportunity. Just realize that the later you make this decision, the more funds you've wasted.

The Bid Go/No Go decision is simply a checklist that involves addressing a series of important issues.

Table 5.2 The Bid Go/No Go Worksheet

Bid Go/No Go issues	Yes	No
1. Is the opportunity aligned with our Strategic and Business Development Plans?		
2. Are we the incumbent? Note: Incumbents with good past performance often have a 90 percent win rate.		
3. If we were the incumbent, did we perform well and did the customer like us?		

4. Do we understand the client's major concerns or issues? Note: These may *not* be explicit in the RFP.		
5. Do we understand all the requirements in the RFP and address them well enough to win?		
6. Do we have a strong team to bid as key personnel on the proposal, both internally and with our teammates?		
7. Does the opportunity make financial sense? Is there adequate ROI?		
8. Do we have the proposal budget we need and the proposal team we need to win?		
9. Can we access the necessary SMEs?		
10. Can we meet the proposal schedule?		

Essential Element PP-3 Budget

An important piece of information for the proposal manager is the available funds he or she has for preparing the proposal. Usually, the Business Development Plan will dictate the total funds allocated for the capture phase and proposal preparation. Going into the proposal phase, the proposal manager should have a clear understanding of the available funds.

The proposal manager should develop a clearly defined budget for the proposal process and keep regular tabs on spending and status.

There are several ways to allocate the available funds. One is to break out an allocation for each lead.

Table 5.3 Sample Proposal Budget Structure

	Labor	**Materials**	**Travel**	**Other**	**Total**
Proposal manager					
Management Volume					
Tech volume					
Cost volume					
Program support					
Production					
Subtotal					

It is important for the program manager to review the schedule to make sure that all actions will be covered by some piece of the budget. In addition, all personnel on the team should be included in one of the line items on the budget. For example, if a SME cost expert is used, his or her labor costs should likely be recognized by the cost volume lead.

The goal is to accurately track the budget, perhaps on a weekly basis, but to keep it as simple as possible so that you can focus your time on the proposal.

Essential Element PP-4 Schedule

The proposal schedule should be created during the capture phase. This allows the team to be aware of any significant schedule concerns prior to making the Bid Go/No Go decision.

In creating the proposal schedule, first determine the five to ten major milestones that must be met, starting with the Draft RFP Release and ending with the contract award. Once you've placed these major milestones in the schedule, you can add in the detail as needed.

There are several reviews that should be conducted throughout the proposal process. Most proposal teams will use three: a Pink team review, a Red team review, and a Gold team review. The purpose of the reviews can vary from industry to industry. Usually the Pink team will review the annotated outline for the proposal to make sure things are on track early in the proposal process. The Red team will review the proposal in its nearly completed form and will ensure that all RFP requirements have been met. The Gold team will do a review of the final proposal and will make sure that the proposed budget provides adequate ROI.

The following is an example of a fairly simple schedule. This example can be used as a starting point, but keep in mind that the exact order of events may vary slightly from effort to effort.

Table 5.4 Proposal Schedule

	Completion date
Draft RFP release	
Review of draft RFP by team	
Bid Go/No Go decision	
Verify proposal team member roles	
Final RFP release	
Final RFP review	

Outline created	
Compliance matrix complete	
Annotated outlines complete	
Pink team reviews	
Draft write-ups complete	
Integration and flow	
Layout complete	
Editing complete	
Red team review	
Final write-ups complete	
Gold team reviews	
Print and assembly	
Delivery	
Orals preparation (if needed)	
Best and final offer and negotiations	
Contract award	

Essential Element PP-5 Compliance Matrix

The compliance matrix is a simple tool but an extremely important tool. Its purpose is to provide a means for verifying that all RFP and Statement of Work (SOW) requirements have been met. Often, the compliance matrix itself is included in the proposal.

At a minimum, if the proposal does not address all requirements in the RFP, and if it does not show an understanding of all requirements in the SOW, then the proposal can be dismissed for noncompliance, and all the hard work and money that went into preparing the proposal is wasted.

There are a couple of approaches to take with respect to the compliance matrix contents, depending upon how much risk you are willing to take. To absolutely be assured of total compliance, every statement in both the RFP and SOW that require the contractor to do something must be addressed. Typically, these are the *shall* statements. But even statements that don't include the word *shall* may actually be a requirement. For example, an administrative requirement that says "black and white printing only is allowed" should be viewed as a requirement.

The best way to build your proposal outline is usually to exactly copy the order of the requirements in the RFP. Table 3.11 shows the structure for a comprehensive compliance matrix. Begin by listing all the RFP requirements in the left-hand column. Under these, list all the SOW requirements. Finally, list any data requirements documents (DRDs) or contract deliverables requirements list (CDRL) items that are required. In addition, the production team may want to add (either in this list or in a separate list) any administrative requirements, such as page counts, layout requirements, font sizes, and so on.

Table 5.5 Compliance Matrix Template

Requirement	RFP or SOW section	Proposal section
	RFP 1.x	1.0
	RFP x.x	1.0

	•	
	•	
	•	
	•	
	RFP x.x	x.x
	SOW 1.x	
	SOW x.x	
	•	
	•	
	•	
	•	
	SOW x.x	
	DRDs	
	CDRLs	

For smaller proposals, or when time does not allow for a detailed compliance matrix, there are a few short cuts that can be considered. But it is important to understand that this often increases the risk of missing a requirement and having the proposal dismissed as noncompliant.

First, the proposal manager may choose to put only the RFP requirements in the compliance matrix. But then, somewhere in the text, it should be made clear that the bidder understands the SOW requirements and will comply with them. This can work well, especially in the case where the SOW is extremely detailed, and the RFP asks the bidder to address only certain points in the prescribed page count.

A second and even riskier approach is to address RFP requirements, but only down to a certain level. Requirements, for example, might go to the x.x.x.x.x level, but the proposal manager may choose to build the compliance matrix down to level x.x.x. This approach also works well for very complex RFPs, especially if the proposal manager would like to put the compliance matrix up front in the executive summary. But just beware of the potential risk for missing a requirement!

Essential Element PP-6 Teammate Selection

There are several reasons for teaming with one or more firms on an opportunity. These include:

- Is the teammate currently an incumbent?

- Does the teammate have a particularly close relationship with the customer?

- Does the teammate have an exceptional reputation in the field or with the customer?

- Do the teammate's core competencies complement yours in such a way as to make the proposal stronger?

- Does the teammate have skills, expertise, knowledge, or processes for a particular requirement or area within the RFP or SOW?

If you decide that it makes sense to have one or more teammates, then there are several steps that need to be taken:

1. Put an NDA in place, if this was not done during the capture phase.

2. Decide on how you will split up the work. There are a couple of ways to do this. The most common is to allocate a certain percentage of total revenue to the teammate. A second method is to use the Compliance matrix to create a work breakdown structure (WBS) based on teammate core competencies.

3. Once you settle on how much and what the teammate will do, you need to create a teaming agreement. The teaming agreement needs to clearly define exactly who does what.

Essential Element PP-7 Key Personnel

Most proposals will ask that the bidder provide names and biographies of the key personnel they plan to use on the contract. There are several issues relating to key personnel that need to be considered for a winning proposal:

- What key personnel does the RFP specifically require?

- What other key personnel should we consider identifying?

- For each of the key personnel we will propose, what attributes would increase our odds of winning? This might include a close relationship with the customer, someone who has specific experience in the customer's agency or group, specific technical or operational experience, and more.

- Who are potential candidates for these key positions, and would they be interested in being bid?

- Can we afford the rates for the key personnel we want to propose?

- Will the customer be excited about who we plan to bid?

Essential Element PP-8 Subject Matter Experts (SMEs)

Subject matter experts are often an important part of proposal preparation. SMEs are used wherever the internal proposal team lacks expertise or time. They can virtually help out in any portion of the proposal phase, but care must be taken to ensure that the proposal budget can be maintained when the SMEs are added.

Once the compliance matrix has been built, the volume leads and Proposal Manager can compare the capabilities and workload for the proposal tem and then determine if outside assistance is needed.

SMEs can come from a number of sources. The first choice is the prime contractor or teammate companies. If that is not sufficient, the proposal manager usually will look outside the team. Again, it is important to adequately account for SME labor and travel in the proposal budget.

Essential Element PP-9 Annotated Outline

An annotated outline should be created once the compliance matrix has been built and the proposal team assignments have been made. An annotated outline begins with building the basic outline for the entire proposal, but then adding enough detail so that the Pink team can tell if the proposal is headed in the right direction.

The proposal outline should follow the RFP requirements as closely as possible. Headings should match the RFP requirements and the RFP headings when feasible. Once the basic outline structure is developed, the proposal manager and volume leads should decide how much detail goes into creating the annotated outline.

For example, the volume lead may decide that each requirement should be a separate subsection and that for each requirement the writer will cover three topics:

1. Understanding of the requirement
2. Our qualifications for meeting the requirement
3. Our approach for meeting the requirement (details on how we will meet the requirement)

The proposal manager and volume leads should also agree to a page count for all pieces of the proposal, an approximate amount of graphics to use, any themes that will be carried through the proposal, and any special formatting or text boxes that might be used.

Essential Element PP-10 Writing

The proposal manager will assign volume leads, who will then need to select writers for various sections of their particular volume. The volume lead is responsible for ensuring these sections get written and that all other consignments of the volume are pulled together and integrated.

To save time and headaches, it is best for the production team to set expectations for the quality of the submitted writing. Providing a simple writer's guide is a great tool (see PP-12 for some ideas to include) for establishing expectations on the quality of the written sections.

It is the writer's responsibility to adequately address the requirements in his or her sections, include appropriate graphics, adhere to any writing expectations specified by the production team, and to generally be consistent with the themes and message of the proposal.

Essential Element PP-11 Layout

There are many choices for a proposal layout. Many firms chose to use a single column format, whereas another popular format is dual column. Some will add highlighted text on the left side of the page to emphasize key points, or will insert text boxes to accomplish the same. Above all, however, proposals should look professional, clean, and uncluttered.

An important decision relating to layout is when to start formatting the text. Often, a *style sheet* is defined by the production team at the start of the proposal phase. The style sheet will show the general layout (which will include the number of columns, font sizes, and margins), how graphics are to be placed and labeled, and more.

It is usually best for the proposal writers to hold off on turning on word processing automation features, such as page numbering and header numbering, text alignment, and automatic creation of the table of contents. These features can cause the writing team to waste significant time and can cause real headaches for the production team when they attempt to integrate the proposal components. It is best for the production team to clearly define the style well ahead of time, and then make it clear how they want text and graphics delivered. Often the production team will not implement these automation features until they pull together the proposal draft for the Red team review.

Essential Element PP-12 Editing and Flow

Editing the proposal text and ensuring that the story line flows from section to section are extremely important elements of putting together a winning proposal. At the start of the proposal phase, the production team should provide writers with a list of basic writing expectations. These might include topics such as:

- Writing in the active voice

- Keeping sentences short and simple

- Use of acronyms

- Punctuation issues (for example, not using too many commas in a single sentence)

Providing these tips up front will usually save editing time, but the production team will still likely need to spend significant time cleaning up the text.

In addition to editing the text, it is important for the finished proposal to not read as though it was written by multiple writers. The proposal evaluators are much more likely to review the proposal favorably if it reads as though it was written by one voice. Again, the editors may be your best source for imposing this one-voice flow, but other reviewers may suffice as well.

Essential Element PP-13 Integration and Page Count

In addition to editing and flow, two other important elements are integration and page count. Integration involves pulling together the entire writer's text, graphics, themes, points to emphasize, and distinguishers or enhancements into a single, integrated volume.

Once the volume is roughly integrated, the production team and volume manager must then make sure that the document meets the required page count. More often than not, the document is too long and requires an iterative process of editing text and graphics until the page count is met. Great care must be taken to ensure that a requirement is not edited to where it is in noncompliance. Likewise, care must be taken so that key points are not edited out accidentally.

Essential Element PP-14 Final Assembly and Print

Upon completion of the reviews and final approval by the proposal manager, the proposal is ready for final assembly and print. The production team should have a checklist ready so that they are absolutely sure that they are providing the correct number of copies, the correct media type, and that the page counts are correct. The checklist should also address the availability of proper equipment and supplies, print services on standby, and any other factors critical to printing and delivering the proposals on schedule.

Essential Element PP-15 Delivery

The production team and proposal manager should decide at the start of the proposal phase how they plan to deliver the proposal to the customer. Customers are tending more and more toward electronic submittal, but this is still not then norm for large or more complex proposals.

Whether the proposals are electronically or physically delivered, the production team should plan for the actual delivery to occur one to two days prior to the RFP delivery date requirement.

Electronic submissions often become difficult on the due date due to clogged networks, and physical deliveries can run into delays due to weather or other unforeseen issues. So, it is best to plan ahead for an early delivery.

Essential Element PP-16 Best and Final Offer (BAFO) and Negotiations

All is not done when the proposal is submitted to the customer. Once the proposals are reviewed and a winner selected, the customer still has several options for awarding the contract. They can simply issue the award and ask for a signature from the winner, or they can announce the winner, but then ask to negotiate on a few points prior to signing the contract.

Another option for the customer is to narrow the potential winners down to a few, then to ask for a best and final offer (BAFO). For a BAFO, they may ask for clarification on certain points or just leave it open for the bidders to offer up their best bid. The bidders can then choose to leave their bids as submitted, or perhaps lower some aspect of cost, or throw in some added feature or service.

Conclusion

Winning new business and growing your company doesn't just happen. To be most effective, it requires direction from the top (Strategic Plan), leadership from the business development team (Business Development Plan), and planning and execution from the capture manager (Capture Plan) and proposal manager (Proposal Plan).

The best practices described by each of the Essential Elements provide a solid foundation for developing these four plans. Also, your company may need to add or remove an element here or there to optimize for your industry or situation. Continuing to optimize your process is both healthy and necessary.

My passion is helping firms succeed with their corporate planning, strategy, and growth processes. I hope this book will help you be successful in these important areas. If you have any questions or comments, please contact me through Encore Business Consulting at www.trustencore.com.

Glossary

BAFO   Best and final offer

BD   business development

CDRL   contract deliverables requirements list

CEO   chief executive officer

CIO   chief information officer

CFO   chief finance officer

CO   contracting officer

COO   chief operations officer

COTR contracting officer technical representative

CP   capture plan

CRM   consumer relationship management

CSO   chief strategy officer

DOD   Department of Defense

DOT   Department of Transportation

DRD   data requirements document

FCC   Federal Communications Commission

G&A   General and Administrative

HLA   high leverage activities

HR   human relations

IT   information technology

NDA   non-disclosure agreement

PM   program manager

PP   Proposal Plan

RFP   request for proposal

ROI   return on investment

SME   subject matter expert

SOW   Statement of Work

SWOT strengths, weaknesses, opportunities, and threats

TA   teaming agreement

WBS   Work Breakdown Structure

About the Author

Don Kelly is a proven senior executive, business leader, and technologist with a twenty-five-year track record of helping businesses succeed. Don brings a unique combination of high-level technology, finance, and business skills and experience from his broad range of executive and management experience. He has served as a CTO for a wireless start-up firm and as a key manager for an operational group within a Fortune 500 firm. He is particularly adept at providing strategic management support, including the areas of strategic planning and positioning, implementing business efficiencies, business development, proposal positioning, developing growth strategies, due diligence, and mergers and acquisitions. Don can be reached at 281-857-6326, www.trustencore.com.

How We Can Help

At Encore Business Consulting, Dr. Kelly provides comprehensive, personalized business management services and advice, specializing in strategy, growth, organization, technology, and operations. Please see our Web site, www.trustencore.com, or call us at 281-857-6326.

Business Management

We provide advice to firms on ways for improving their efficiency and, thus, their profitability. This advice often spans across inter-related areas that include near-term and long-term strategies, policies and procedures, positioning and planning, growing the business, the use of available resources, the best use of manpower, and a critical assessment of industrial relations, market position, and services offered. In addition, Dr. Kelly can augment your executive team for the purpose of mentoring someone in a new role, during surge periods, assisting with a reorganization, or in cases of staffing shortages.

Strategic Planning

Encore works with executive teams in strategic planning development and implementation. The result of this process is to produce a concise, winning business strategy, including defining the business purpose, short and long-term business goals, core competencies, markets and opportunities, SWOT analyses, and action plans for implementing the plan. Executives have found our process to be extremely valuable for creating or refining the strategic plan, and, even more importantly, in getting consensus from the entire executive team.

Strategic Growth

Growth is best achieved through the close alignment of business development to corporate strategy. We help companies in creating this alignment. We also assist in identifying major opportunities, developing strong proposal teams, providing subject matter expertise, formulating strategies, identifying unique distinguishers and innovations, and performing cost analyses. In addition, we support Pink, Red, and Gold team reviews, assist in creating or reviewing annotated outlines, assist with building compliance matrices, provide subject matter expertise, ensure requirements are adequately addressed, help in refining the unique distinguishers and innovations, and assist with proposal planning.

Acknowledgments

First, I'd like to thank my wife, Joy, for supporting me throughout the long process of pulling together this book. Her enthusiasm and encouragement along the way was a tremendous inspiration for me!

Debbie Lee Parmley led the effort in getting much of the information pulled together in a readable manner and formatted for the book. Thanks so much, Debbie.

I also really appreciate the peer reviewers that looked at my content and provided many valuable suggestions for improvements. Much thanks to Randy Parmley, Paul Withington, Ken Kelly, Paul Maine, Dr. Joy Kelly, and Pavan Rajagopal.

Download Instructions for Free Templates

To download free templates and other information associated with this book, please go to my Web site: www.trustencore.com.

For the templates that require a password, please enter the following:

strategy

References

[i] http://www.usatoday.com/money/smallbusiness/columnist/abrams/2004-05-06-success_x.htm

[ii] http://www.sba.gov/smallbusinessplanner/plan/getready/SERV_SBPLANNER_ISENTFORU.html

[iii] http://www.businessweek.com/smallbiz/news/coladvice/ask/sa990930.htm

[iv] http://www.businessweek.com/smallbiz/news/coladvice/ask/sa990930.htm

[v] http://www.businessknowhow.com/startup/businessfailure.htm

[vi] http://smallbiztrends.com/2008/04/startup-failure-rates.html

[vii] http://www.sba.gov/smallbusinessplanner/plan/getready/SERV_SBPLANNER_ISENTFORU.html

[viii] Tony Jeary, *Strategic Acceleration* (Philadelphia, PA: Vanguard Press, 2009)

[ix] Jack Welch, *Winning* (New York, NY: HarperCollins Publishing, 2005)

[x] www.fbo.gov

[xi] www.input.com

[xii] Robert Bradford and J. Peter Duncan, *Simplified Strategic Planning*, (Worcester, MA: Chandler House Press, 2000).n